Boiling Hot

Boiling Hot

Poems by

Nancy Anne Miller

Kelsay Books

ISBN: 978-1-947465-95-4

Kelsay Books
Aldrich Press
www.kelsaybooks.com

For the great aunts at Hillcrest:

Alice, Suzannah, (Suzie), and Gladys (Jack) Hutchings

Acknowledgements

I would like to thank the editors of the following journals for publishing my poems as well as the Bermuda Arts Council for helping to fund my first chapbooks.

Agenda: "Seahorse," and "Snakeskin"
Ambit: "Punt," and "Ship Clock"
Anomaly: "Recorded"
Art Ascent: "Words that Curl and Curve"
BM: "Happy Birthday Nation,"
Commentaries: "Not Italian," and "My Father's Ship"
Interviewing the Caribbean: "Coral Gardening," and "Fire on
    Front Street"
Magma: "Olivetti"
Orbis: "Brain Coral,"
Poetry Pacific: "Seahorse," and "Olivetti"
Postcolonial Text: "Antique Star Map," "Boiling Hot," "Buoy,"
Poui: "Antique Star Map," "Boiling Hot," "Rudder," "Sea Horse,"
    and "Swimming Lessons"
Southword: "Side Saddle"

The following poems were published in the chapbooks:

The Sun in Three Countries (Bermuda Arts Council 2003):
    "Portuguese," "Leisure," and "Chintz"
Hurricane Season (Bermuda Arts Council 2007): "English Sky,"
    "Mad Cow Disease," "Wheel of Fortune," and "Holy Day"
Maiden Voyage (Bermuda Arts Council 2009): "Bathing Caps,"
    and "Hands"

Contents

Happy Birthday Nation

Lure

About the Author

One's homeland is not a geographical convention, but an insistence of memory and blood.

—Marina Tsvetaeva

Punt

Antique Star Map

Round as a crystal ball,
one might turn to find a path,
hold in one's hand, cup
a drop in the ocean. This one

has a star in the middle, like
a Bermuda Sand Dollar, I
would find on Coral Beach,
the tides washed over, spent.

A pin cushion where precise
points prick the dark. A child's
circle of marbles, large planets
knock out smaller ones: taws

hit peewees. The nineteenth century
one is full of flying figures, a Sistine
Chapel for ship captains, where one
looks up to feel the muscle of

myths ripple the heavens.
Capricorn's bow and arrow,
a shipmate's sextant used to negotiate
the skies, to find a seaworthy mark.

Up-Bringing

Replicates the long evolution
of life, the sea sheds one scale
after another as a wave falls off
its cusp, drops down in the sand.

Where our footprints sink, sink
deeper into the moment we walked
upright. Put our hand above
our brow in the harsh light

to block the sun, like a cedar
shutter on a limestone Bermuda
cottage, or a salute back to
the ocean for bringing us here.

Seahorse

No need for wings or legs
in the buoyant tide of the ocean.

Like the *f* hole in a cello
where the music seeps through.

Miscellaneous notes in the waves
symphony. Shaped like a pick I

used to clean Lacquer's hooves,
removed earth from the iron

shoe so he could soar higher
when sweat poured down

his back, salty as the ocean's
surf, smelling of the undersea.

Words that Curve and Curl

Words that curve and curl
from the sea, the tide, dampness,
get into everything. The seaweed
clings to your calf when you
walk out of the water, like varicose
veins as you return to land legs.

Words that curve and curl, like the conch,
Allamanda petals, the roundabout
where Mobylettes, Zundaps, Morris
Minors swish by, fish in a current.
Words that curve and curl, collect
the island dead center as in the eye

of a hurricane. Don't sit up straight
on the page like for a class at B.H.S.
Overflow into the world like when I
jumped overboard in Paget Harbour
caused rivulets which rocked boats,
anchors wanting to tipsy into the ocean.

Ship Clock

for Nancy Christina Hutchings

I hold it up to cousin Tina, the Westclox
wall clock in a St. Georges supply
store and say it is like a porthole
with the sea lapping its blue rim,

will keep BDA time when I am in
America. The second hand like
the shadow on a sundial at Hillcrest
circling, cuts light, sharp as a shark's fin.

A Pinocchio nose as the day
elongates its boundary of truth.
Where is it? Not here, nor
there. I remember the ship clock

at Greystones, turns in the glass
case, an earring, time's immediate
jewel. Multiple bells ring, the ocean's
ripples when an anchor strikes deep.

Bathing Caps

My aunts tuck hair into white
bathing caps like a novice's ritual.
The curling surf does not allow
rivalry as the tide lets down locks.

Their torso hangs beneath them
like a snail's body outside a shell.
The tide twirls conch like
as the rubber seals them deaf.

I shout at them, but they
will not hear me. Docile as dolphins,
peaceful babies, momentarily
wrapped in the ocean's calm.

Recorded

She preferred the days the light
shimmered off the snow like
on a South Shore beach, Bermuda.

Watched the Tompkins men
shovel the path, the blur of
ice over their shoulder a wave,

one bobbed in as a child for hours.
Or like a towel thrown on one's back
while walking out from the water.

The white, white sleet billows
around the 1814 saltbox house,
a mast pulling it into the deep.

The non-negotiable horizon, driven
away like the bright sun made it so
as her sea captain ancestor recorded.

Sums

What do you know of sums
when the angel fish adorns a one
pound island note? Air bubbles,
coinage from a scaled purse,
glittery as a sequined bag.

What of the Mathematician's toil?
When you learn subtraction, addition
by the in, out of the ocean. When you
learn to count collecting sand dollars
in a child's pail, and they are

a thousand years old. What can you
know of savings? When rain water is
caught in the bottom line of a gutter off
white washed roofs. Amounts always
rationed, a glass half empty, never half full.

Punt

I have to notice the white
three leveled bookshelf I
order is like a wooden punt,

blunt, simple, occupies space
without notice. Remember
sitting in the middle of mine,

rowing Ely's Harbour. Each
oar pulling up water like
an open book with clear pages.

Handles forming an arrowhead
either way. Out to sea, back
to the beach. I was thick in

the plot of the afternoon,
my back like any binding
to a text having to endure

the opening, the closing of
the strokes against the tide,
the weight of the full meaning.

Buoy

If you are going to leave your island,
better do it on a ship, where you see
the water between the dock and your
liner extend into the crease of waves,

open into an accordion. Feel your
heart roll back, forth, a buoy tethered to
the wharf. If you must leave your country,
better a seaborne way, the tilt of

swells rocks you inconsolable as
in a nanny's crib. Better than by
plane where through a tiny window
like your diving mask of youth, the hook

isle drops away, the sinker you watch
disappear into harbour waters when
you fished off Paget Ferry. Better
a boat that stole many an ancestor into

the blue, so when you pour the sludge
of Earl Grey from a silver teapot,
muddy water from an elephant trunk,
it holds all memories that slosh inside, still.

Glow Worms

Like the moon which calls them up,
they glow with a see through light,
resemble beached condoms I found
washed up on the South Shore.

The females do their circular
dance, mimic the orgasmic
ripple, the tide of one wave breaks,
over into, becomes another.

Their dervish twirls, the earth's spin,
call the males from below who
spiral into rings, whirl around planets.
Eggs, sperm exchange a green

Flash Gordon moment, the spark
of quick sex. Wings of an Icarus
torn off before falling back through sky,
glow worms descend the black hole dark.

Rudder

Like a Good Friday Kite
which flew too far out of
sky bound realms, the mast
and sail tattered on the seabed is

finally at rest. Rows of
barnacles, the nails screwed
in to keep it still, steady.
We all want to find permanence.

A ship captain relative was
buried at sea in an un-floatable
coffin. The white breaking surf
parted open as it entered the deep.

The only wings seen to rescue
him although sea fans flourished
on the top, like one his widow waved
back, forth, a rudder to direct her grief.

Old Whaling Church Clock

A black face, brass numbers, bits of stars
break, collapse into a supernova circle.

The hands, two sticks which rub together
until dawn's fire ignites. Tower shines like

a candle at night, wax ones captain's wives put
in bay windows, small, intimate lighthouses.

Each chime a piano chord struck against
the hour's refrain when women harmonized

lives to the quiet. The sanctuary below large
as a mammal's belly where the organ's ivory

keys resonate with the whale's traveling song.
They bore ambergris, oil, up from where bio-

luminescence glows, and their waterspout was
a wick full of light on a widow's lantern.

Unclaimed

The whale's nubby skin
in the video of underwater life
off Bermuda reminds me of
a giant corrugated pickle. One
floating in a jar, tastes sea salty.

The place where no sun shines,
the deep, deep makes what
floats by unclaimed by shadow,
the weight of which locates,
instead adrift, bits ghostly.

This un-named jellyfish
looks like a plastic hat a woman
would wear to keep her bob safe
from rain, keep the wave in it. And
this burst of light from one

bioluminescent form, a Van Gogh
Sunflower, or the photographer's
strobe. This eel buckling,
a loosened belt. Tongue, the clasp
that couldn't hold the currents.

Amulet

The iron canon next to the shipwreck,
with large wheels, long narrow barrel
is an elephant's head, cannot forget.
The sea is history! as Walcott said.

This ship, half a cantaloupe scooped
out from the ocean's appetite, hunger.
Angelfish fly over it, waver the blue,
heavenly beings soothe the site.

This island collects wrecks the way
a matriarch woman adds a charm
to her gold bracelet, displays them
at the club. The dark map of reefs,

in relief like reading braille. Many vessels
downed, tracking a lantern on a cow,
an amulet, like a saint's medal one clasps
to pray for safe passage. Bleeds light into

the dark, a religious stigmata to coax
belief, while the boat is stripped as it
descends, mast shredded, removed. It
rocks, rests on the seabed, still as an anchor.

Flip, Flop

Was what the snapper did on the dock
in the shallow pool of harbour water,
like a ballet slipper un-sprung
from its shoe tree, tries to flip, flop

off. That is how I feel on my return,
gills open in layered fans to find
the direction of the ocean's breeze.
Fish's eye looks up to the sky as it lies

there, mistakes it for the sea. Suspended
in the sliver of the water's silvery
memory. The other pupil blocked
with the patch of the grainy cement.

My vision, one sided, too, Bermuda,
America. Never combine, flip, flops,
contorts as I too drop off, convulse
from Bermuda's fishhook shape terrain.

She Brought the Sea Inside

for Nancy Walters Valentine

Our homes in her fiberglass panels,
Sargasso Seaweed, bivalve mollusk
shells, coral sand caught in the swing

of a door, opened up the ocean's chambers.
A zigzag triptych screen, a testimony to
our faith in turning turquoise waters.

Arranged the details like a wave had just
tilted them so. What we knew from
swimming underwater, what we felt as

the tide tipped up and in on Windsor
Beach, rushed to shore the ocean's
luminous loot. *She brought the sea inside!*

Allowed light to filter through the purple
sea fan's porous hand, unable to hold
it tight, illuminating our real treasure,

next to all the other household goods:
cedar chests and Chippendale chairs,
the Spode, silver, and Waterford crystal.

Unending

If I told you sleeping in an 1814
house with slanted roof was like
being under half a jib, the chestnut
beam at ceiling's edge, the boom.

If I told you that the fire going
out was the sun's cinders on the sea
waves' cool edge, all crackle and spit
in the dark. *Red sky at night…*

If I told you our ancestors
wrote our story as sea captains
wrote mine, each line a horizon
with tilts and heaves unending.

If I told you the snow was a torn sail
shredded in the bluffs of a storm
circling, as its triangle of blown
pride disappears into the vast blue.

The Only News

The sun is a nun, face shrouded by clouds,
veils of ordination. She tries to walk lightly
on water with her silver feet. The wind is up,

turns the palm tree leaves, like ribs of
sunken boats in its tide. I sit under a parasol,
spokes like a wheel, the day spins around.

The only news is the weather, gusts giving
limestone houses a shove, rattling shutters,
spiraling down chimneys to make them

stand up straight. What can I face in such
buoyancy? The tide unrolls a slippery carpet
into the sea. What can I know in such change?

Ship-Wrecked

It was a sea worthy trunk,
steely, typical of one shipped
to college with rackets, l.p.
records, extra Shetland sweaters.

But mine didn't end up there,
rather birthed in a storage warehouse,
not just riding the waves
between home and university.

But mine didn't end up there,
because a father out of work,
couldn't pay the monthly fee,
and so my possessions descended,

fell into some unknown under-
tow of nameless places: thrift
shops, tag sales, a pawn broker's
window. Like my ancestor's

going to Bermuda, being ship-
wrecked freed me. I lost
most of what brought me here.
The cargo that could have sunk me.

At Sea

Always, the wave spreads
transparent as those plastic pads
I would indent with an attached pen.

Then pull up to tumble all words
off like shaking crumbs from
a tablecloth. The same way

the tide pulls back, leaves
a shiny surface except for
the pebbles, shells, plankton

which can't be washed away.
I want to write that poem,
the one nothing can erase,

no matter the suction, the pull
back, the language clinging
to shore that won't be lost at sea.

Boiling Hot

Side Saddle

She sits like a mermaid in
a side saddle, a kind of
extra dish to compliment
the main. Dangerous not

to use both legs, be off
balance, tilt the horse
one way with too heavy
a burden, a sack thrown

over a hook, Pegasus with
one wing. Like a seal lunges
towards the frothy surf of
the mane. The spread thighs

saved for one occupation,
or the other where birth
stirrups come to mind. Let
her post in synch with ups,

downs, slip the soft slide
canter, shoe horns her
forward, the full throttle
gallop, her power out of

the gates, she leans into
the reins' horizon line, pulls
the snaffle bit in the horse's
mouth: wish boning her will.

Boiling Hot

She rubs the silver pot, with
Gorham's polish as if her genie
was inside, would waft out from
the steam island tea makes

in such a humid climate. Prepares
triangle sandwiches, lops off
dark crusts that heap on the kitchen
counter as if caterpillars crawled out

from frilly lettuce leaves, like sea's
wavy rim, the silk cap sleeves on
smocked dresses made for the misses.
Arranges a square like the cross

intersection of the Amen Corner in Paget,
a treacherous passage through.
Dons white gloves used for church
and to serve among the fair English.

Watches their skin turn earth brown,
the harsh light claiming a geography
of persons the empire sent across
the world. The British sunrise on

every commoner's door back in
London, an unblinking watchful eye,
a fan spread wide open to
cool down boiling hot countries.

Chintz

Curtains hang to the side of
the windows fluted as columns.

Make the garden-view, the inner
sanctuary of a temple. Edges of

the hibiscus bud are shaded in
with the skill of a cartographer

lining maps. There is leeway for
the changing tides around a point.

The stems of the plants grow up
the stiff fabric. A river finding the way,

ready to be explored. Birds sit
oddly as shoaled boats, heads with

eyes, beaks turn into the room,
small as handheld compasses.

Counting Elephants

The one the binocular spots has two pencils stubs
in its mouth, yet, it is from a plane flying over statisticians

count elephants in Africa. Large grey leathery hides
are the colour of erasers, nothing can be rubbed out,

forgotten in deeply furrowed minds. Trunks thrust water
over bodies to refresh memory, tracks are embedded in muddy

banks with legs so thick, men make stools from them,
each stride, a place to sit, dwell. Volunteers use laptops

to spot them, a special film leaves marks, oil streaks where
they float up out of the dark of the screen, the dreamy

effervescent blue of underwater life glows to protect,
warn. While poachers seek tusks, hooks to pull such

a large catch down. This one moves ears forward
into a large hearted valentine as it faces the camera.

Traffic Signals

On the old Morris Minor station wagon,
raise a left, right blinker: wings sprout
on a cherub, so small for a curvy body.

Its orange luminous as a chameleon
tongue against a British Racing Green
surface. Hard to discern, but not at 25

miles per hour on Middle Road, Paget
in the 1950's. Just another bud in
the semitropical landscape like a bird

of paradise bloom. The African Jamaican
on the Mobylette drops his hand down
as if an anchor, fingers the air softly

like feeding snappers bread off Hodson's
Ferry before turning, leans his shoulders
in. Anglo Bermudian, Miss Grey rings

the bicycle bell on her Humber Bike, a wee
tad pole swims the air as she pedals a hill
on Lovers Lane, looks as if she climbs

evolutionary steps when pumping hard. Beak
shaped flags at the top of a boat's mast, give
terse directions, white sheets billow below,

a hen's plumage of feathers. I sit under
the Sunfish sails, a large Bermuda Triangle,
signals I will disappear into the entire afternoon.

At the Club

It is the ruffled clouds above in blue
that are like childhood surf, clothed
un-clothed her as it rushed into South
Shore. Lake Waramaug can only be
a steely flat pan she sifts for memory.

The large inflated trampoline on the outer
rim of the roped in water tempts,
a donut cools on a shelf. The speedboat
with a dark prow is Woody Woodpecker,
flaps through the calm. *So American!*

she says under her breath. Mexican workers
lay stone paths like pilgrims, remind her of
Portuguese in Bermuda planting hibiscus rows
at the club for privacy. Spoke their mother
tongue to each other, to keep all members out.

Portuguese

Your homeland lies between
England and Africa. Here we
place you between us,

a latitude and longitude for
our distances. Your presence
became a purgatory where

light and dark comingle.
Your holy days fill our streets,
blur hedges into paths for

mysteries. A silent suspended
cross pulls bodies into a rosary.
You turn over our idle earth,

give it back to Mary. She
showers our long neglect
with rows of fragrant flowers.

Hands

at Stratford College, Virginia.

Mary Jane raised her hand,
placed it in the air as if the maid
might pick it up too, an extra fork
she clears from the dining room table.

Regina lifts hers as well like slipping
it into an evening glove,
time to retire from dinner,
after coffee is served to all.

The black women with backs to the wall,
wore white ones, not to touch
the plates, leave fingerprints
as they tidied up the mess.

At Christmas a server sang Silent Night.
The girls applauded loudly. The flurry
of palms hitting palms were like
doves released in the air for peace.

Selfie

Bermuda takes a selfie of itself
every night when Gibbs Hill
Lighthouse flashes Weegee style

into the dark. Rays of light form
a Byzantine halo like the Statue of
Liberty's crown welcomes above

NYC harbour. Contemplative in
the day, a French Nun's veils trail,
beams barely discernible in the breeze,

except to the eye of the wayfarer keen
to see a Don Quixote windmill on
every horizon, immensely approachable.

Piggly Wiggly Camera

Fudji Instant Max 8

Like it is a hog for all the views
here on my semitropical isle.

The belly button lens,
everything seen tribal,

connects to the umbilical cord,
squats with the strap curling

like a piglet's tail. I take pictures
through its greedy eye. Think

of the island food store Piggly Wiggly
nourishing Bermudians. Like this Polaroid

feeds me the crumbs of moments.
Piggly Wiggly all the way home.

In the Semi-Tropics with a Venetian Blind

Slices a blank page into lines for
a composition class at BHS.

The multi lines a sea captain hallucinates
as he stares into the blank horizon .

A Japanese lantern I pull up, hoist
a stiff Victorian slip full of whale bones.

In Venetia it was good to have straight
lines, while watching gondolas tipsy-ing.

Swimming Lessons

The poet from the B.V.I.
said she never learned to
swim even though
shorelines with their frilly

bathing skirts beaches are
open to all islanders. Her
genes remember the fear
of water, ancestors held

in the mouth of a ship
the ocean tried to expunge
while it heaved and rolled.
Vomit them up through

the cracked veneer of
the vessel's curved lips.
The masters never allowed
lessons lest slaves would

flee. Who saw the surf
as chains, a net pulling
them down under. Not
clouds of frothy light,

one could ride. Not where
a body could float, ride
the tide's whims, touch,
un-touching the shore.

Coral Gardening

The divers are angels
as they descend, air bubbles
the silent speech blurbs the sea
demands, are filled with blank awe.

Reefs have made them wordless,
afloat in a buoyant sky. These
coral gardeners bring trays
of young coral like chicks, attach

them to tent structures, homes
for ocean refugees. A temporary house
to grow long fingers, to stroke,
sift the blue for the sun's gold.

Too many dying from heat
the bright fans of angelfish can't cool.
Burns them into a nuclear fallout,
left in heaps, bleached skulls, helmets

in an underwater post war site.
Where schools of Jacks ban together,
move, like group torpedoes shot at
a target un-seeable in blinding light.

Fire on Front Street

The three story buildings are
the only sense of a mountain
we have, smoke billows as if
from a volcano like our first

breath of life as the isle was birthed
into the sea. Clouds, like parachutes,
air bags released in an accident
float up, away from the city line.

It is all snakes and ladders on Ber-News
periscope footage. The ladders tilt
to windows, the hoses, serpents.
People rub their eyes to see better

or to wake up in Bermuda's early hours.
The fire men spray water like flashlights,
the blaze jumps in and out of the luminous
path, Gombeys dancing on Front Street.

I hear peeping frogs on the video:
a charm or a talisman rattled for
heaven to bring rain. Bermudian
voices calm, not excited, soothe,

occasionally laugh in front of disaster:
Quo fata ferunt! deep in our soul. Palm
trees arc taller, spread fronds, Corinthian
arches to hold up our morning sky.

Honey Dipper

The dipper on the breakfast
buffet table at Salt Kettle House,
on the side of a bowl swells
with honey, looks like a bee

with orbed stripy shape and
a long stinger. Rumpelstiltskin's
spinning wheel spins straw
into gold. Drips light.

Rapunzel lowers her locks
into my early a.m. So, I might
climb out of my slumber, get
into the buzz of the day.

Because

Because I've been there
in the wee rain-splashed village,
been where the last drop

falls into the cup of a hand,
where ale brims over, spills
onto the bar's cedar table.

The town routed by puddles,
wet mouths opening, drink in
sky, suck it away into ground.

The smudgy finger prints
of water on the window,
sliding down, losing

their grip. I've been in that
town, North Devon or
County Antrim, where

the cobbled streets look
like tears hardened,
stopped. Where the villagers

stump their toe, and trip
from old losses that rivers
can't float, don't carry away.

English Sky

The man with the smile
full of piano keys,
that man is playing
his island drum
on the road over the Thames.
To give the English sky

drizzling a sad song,
a small ringing sun.
The tinny metallic sound
echoes in the street,
structured with a rainbow's curve
over the traffic moving

in brief starts and stops.
The music from the oil can
warms the passerby
caught between the threaded bars,
holding up the bridge with
the taut strings of a Spinet's interior.

Holy Day

The tourists descend cautiously,
walk the cobblestone path, descend
down into Clovelly, like stepping
on eggs near the Easter coloured houses.

Balance their ice cream cones,
jugglers with sticks and balls,
eat it before the sky melts
strawberry in the sky.

The only way back up
is on a donkey's back,
to keep the holiday light,
not turn it into a burden.

Leisure

Time just kicks by
all horizontal in
the can can
chorus line of a wave,

Small events attain
importance like buoys
in a sucking slow sand
sea where no one

fights for their life.
White frothy sunscreen
turns bodies into mummies
as the heat erases faces

made calmly ancient.
Decay aimlessly in
the head to toe, regal
sun king silk of a tan.

Wheel of Fortune

The train shuttles along
with the same sound
as the cards hitting
the spokes of my Humber bicycle.

I clothes-pinned them
onto the fender
to make a motoring noise
as I peddled down Lover's Lane.

A locomotive comes
from another direction,
bearing down with
spinning roulette wheels.

Cars pass by each other
in a blur of windows,
a deck shuffled
between the dealer's hands.

Mad Cow Disease

If only our mothers had
come with their own
geography of dark and

light places. Patched black
and white as these Devon
cows. Their moods wandered

at random. Udders appearing
swollen as a 'Portuguese
Man O' War' stinging. Or

soft as a glove that
stroked our silky hair
while we were nursing.

Happy Birthday Nation

Happy Birthday Nation

Like popcorn popping on summer's
hot skillet, dreams burst or grow from
a seed into strong stalks bejeweled by the sun.

The sky is a banner, the country's
flag of stars, stripes as firecrackers
write its freedom story on the night.

Quivers, like a picnic tablecloth shaken from
crumbs. Our celebratory graffiti which
includes the moon and mars beyond

before dimming. Candles blown out
while we pack up, load the car full, ready
to fast forward into the sparks of autumn.

Not Italian

Not Italian like a man sitting in
a sleeveless Tee shirt, his chest
hangs down, a ham strung between
the handles of a string market bag.

No, not Italian with the smell
of garlic in a mouth, its
claw scratching through; ones
left on a kitchen table, a secret

ritual to the saint of missing
teeth. Nor Italian with a Mary
medal on a chain, going back and
forth, a cable lift between

right and left pecks. Nor
keeping her on a front
lawn in a stone arch, bent
head emerging like a turtle,

the mother of slow prayer.
But, yes, Italian like Roma was
not built in a day, buildings
with their open infrastructure all

over Bermuda, cement and steel
Coliseums. The name Milani,
a thousand years, a thousand years
seen everywhere on all island roads.

My Father's Ship

Came in, in Hartford CT where it is berthed.
The glass ship building, cloud sails blew
across, and the sky crinkled waves over.

To celebrate, we eat at Honiss's Ocean Bar
below hard pavement. Sit in a wooden booth
small as a punt, fork ready as King Neptune.

Order Jacks, Bream, Pompano, I once lifted
off hooks, held fins down, like island Kiskadee wings.
Order oysters small as an evening purse, find

a rough pearl inside, a tiny spare earring. Waiters
hover, polite as Cunard porters on our voyage to
New York. Framed daily newspapers, full of

American success stories, surround like T.V.'s
always on. Squared portholes below sea level, to view
a world where my father's see-through ship arrived.

Out and About

I think I am at a five star
restaurant when I read labels
on canned dogfood: salmon
with asparagus, duck with wild rice.

When I pay for it I am told
to put my card in a slot because
it has a chip. It looks like a tongue
stuck out for a medical exam.

The shop owner says it is for
added security. I laugh, think
how we still leave bills, personal
mail in our mailboxes on the road.

Unlocked, without keys or digital
apparatus. Their covered wagon
shape, white and curved, remind
me of when life was wild, open, free.

Age Appropriate

The sound of the banjo, the hiccup
start-up chords of a brand-new country,
snapping suspenders with scurrying fidgety

hands. Baroque Era, music as anti-depressant
before pills, before mood swings were recorded,
French Horns bullying gloom away.

The sixties when hippies lay guitars on
their laps, decapitated bodies with a large
belly button, grew their hair long for

extra strings. Beach Boys' high notes
peaking in waves, tongue surfing through,
the thrill of riding a long note, not falling.

How the Statue of Liberty Came to America.

A bad hair day, the Statue of Liberty's
crown looks punkish, pulled up into spikes.
Did we ever notice the girl is carrying
a torch, about to set something alight?

An article in The Daily Beast said she
was originally Muslim, bound for a life
near the Suez Canal. Appropriately dressed,
peasant's scarf, baggy clothes, the kind of garb

something from the old country could be
smuggled under. More the refugee look, an ad
for participants. Now she is metallic, military,
Joan of Arc without the horse. Or is the Don

Quixote Windmill, crown the propellers,
an impossible dream! Had to change identity
to come North, like most who come across
borders, Anglified themselves. Angled life

with the *Fie! Fie! Fie!* fire of an immigrant. Her
back is turned on America, she looks out
to sea with her torch teeming into a brush,
touches clouds to white out whatever is necessary.

Unsmiling

Swimmers bob the Jersey
Shore, clutch onto bathing
rings, look like workers
coming up out of manholes.

A friend rides a surfboard
as if on a Chevy's fender,
sharp as a shark's fin, disappears
into the wave's tunnel, mimics

concrete ones that swirl into
New York. The sound of traffic
in the cement circular byways
resonates like inside a conch

I picked up on South Shore,
full of the ocean's tremours.
There the tide came in, out.
A glassy toenail painted

over, over in the perfection
of leisure. Here, the Statue of
Liberty rises, a beached mermaid,
the turquoise water has turned

to armour. Unsmiling, defiant,
with the pathos of a Giotto angel
her spiked crown of thorns
bleeds the dark. Choice is sacrificial.

As American As

My hair is pulled up, stiffened
into a Mohawk, I am next to a spikey
statue of liberty as I sit at my hairdresser's,
wait for the colour to take. She

is from Bosnia and talks about how
she never learned to bake pies
in her country. Likewise in Bermuda
cassava pie was not made of New

England's two crusted clam shells,
edges curving into the rivulets of
a wave. I never saw such either, nor
heard the boast of women on how they

are made. It is Thanksgiving and the PBS
programme on Pilgrims shows how
peace was made between them
and a mercantile colonist by the slaughter

of the later. His decapitated head
displayed astride Plymouth's central
post, like our lady of the harbour's
torch held high to welcome all. In

the huts of puritans, pies were baked,
simply made, heat escaping through
slices in the crust, wispy as the first
strands of hair on an infant's skull.

Heat

They bring the heat with them
as they roar down Nettleton
Hollow, a motorcycle emits blasts
like a human passing wind.

The muffler, a hot cigar,
drops ashes rudely,
in the bucolic green hills
as it emits a sooty trail.

Their loud *clap! clap!* of thunder,
is such a summer sound.
The noise just before a down-
pour, then the quiet they leave behind.

Puzzle

The large jug of maple syrup is like
a can of gasoline one might use
to fill a car tank. The silky liquid
colour the same golden brown.

Born from the incendiary season
of autumn when trees roar fire,
like someone dumped fuel and
lit a match to burn out foliage.

We humans want warmth. Pour
sticky sweetness over pancakes
in the morning, make treacly suns.
We humans want warmth. Go to

beaches, burn the absentee space
of bathing suits into our flesh.
Naked bodies now a graphic jigsaw
piece for the larger puzzle we fit.

Olivetti

If I could line letters up
like soldiers, the way they
are assembled in my Olivetti
typewriter with white shiny

cadet hats I would. If I could
neaten the process of writing,
make it precise, orderly,
ceremonial I would. Silver

rungs rise up, salute
each letter as they
march onto the page. If
I could make my writing

not skip a beat and turn
back to form a new line
of thought at the sound
of a bell while I throw

the carrier back. A private
switching her gun from
her left to right shoulder,
I would, if I could.

Accord

When I bought the accordion
from the old secondhand shop
in Danville, VA and opened it,
it was like shuffling cards in

my hand. A book with notes
and sounds, the active verbs
in sentences I would never master.
The buttons, un-fasten-able for

music-less fingers. A topsy
turvy stairway, opens
so one can escape, climb
to sky or down to earth, then

closes into a heavy purse
to carry. A pump to release
extra air, the kind a Beethoven
Sonata carries, or the gasp

in the jig tune jam of the Irish.
A Polish waltz where partners
part separate, unite, within
the starched crease of tradition.

Lure

Brain Coral

The forsythia covered with snow
looks like the grooved brain coral
I would swim above in turquoise waters.

Wallace Stevens said one should have the mind
of winter. I come from an island where
we pay no mind to what we can't be teased

with. I refuse these April fool tricks,
the gas light shifts of nature. I choose
to see the ice turn branches into a canvas

of Cy Twombly's scribbles. The hint
of beginnings, the urge to scrawl,
suggest what is not, by what is. His

back, forth to Rome, Lexington full
of histories must have made him in love
with the somersault of turns. The spring

coil of time like the inside of a clock gone
awry, the cusp curving into itself to form
a nest where something is birthed.

The outline of trees against the sandy sleet
has the pull of tide, the seaweed left on
a beach suggests the teeming life underwater.

The marooned synapses in the skull not
connecting to conclude, flourish, just
the twiggy-ness of intuition white hot.

It Ain't Over Until It's Over

The trees have thrown
down their branches,
like toys in a tantrum
for the chilling air to stop.

Place roadblocks on dirt
roads, levies to allow
the flow of mud to slide
down hills in increments.

The apple trees in the orchard,
are Sumi wrestlers, all ribcage
and shoulder muscle to lift
the earth up. The lake cracks

into scales of a trout flopping,
flailing to prove it's alive. The calf
on the hills raises its newborn
pink face into the blue, a bud.

Lure

Unopened Tulip buds line up in front
of the stonewall, in front of
the colonial house like lipsticks,
eager to adorn, beautify.

The dandelions in the farm
pasture have blasted yellow to
white hot. Their circle dots
the eye on spring's early days.

And the leaves on the young
oak are lures on branches,
sinkers I put on fish lines, to take
it further into the deep blue.

The stuff of ghost trees
in Mexico: pictures of the dead,
chimes, charms, hung
to bring the departed back to life.

Pitchfork

Who says lightning can't strike twice?
Here, the maple fills out with the same
luminosity it did, last spring.

And the forsythia buckles with light,
rolling in circles across
the greening ground. Who says?

When I split open each May,
the fault line of such feeds my heart
like a pitchfork to the sun.

July Fatigue

As in the daylilies droop, as if
dripping heat, the panting tongues
of dogs before the stem, flower
stiffen into a hand hexed against

the cold. Now the Black Eyed
Susan appear, nailed down suns,
tacked, an eye bruised from
light stares blankly up. In the far

field foliage turns at edges, thumbed
pages of a much-read book, flicked,
to find the season's story before
it falls into a deconstructed text.

Who Knew?

The Maple's summer was so complex,
reveals its geography of sun,
no longer viridian green, but multi-
coloured: fuchsia red, cadmium yellow,

sienna orange. Each leaf the season's topography:
contours of squalls, wind vibrations,
humidity levels recorded like a sinner stands
at the gates, all intentions now known. Who knew

a pile of decomposed leaves would remind
me of Mrs. Brett's mare Ever Dear? Dropping
road apples on Lovers Lane, the smell strong
as late autumn orchards. Who knew I would

think crumbled foliage, sawdust from grandpa's
cedar sawmill in Hamilton where wood
was pared down, shaped into planks for
chairs, chests, taken aboard a ship

on the ocean's tipsy sea. Like this leaf
peaks into variegated edges, inverted
curves undulating as a wave rises, crests,
the sweep up as all the rest falls down.

Short Season

It is too short a season to have a pool,
cousin Lisa says. I think of the ones in
Bermuda mimicking the turquoise ocean,
diving boards stuck out like tongues

collect rain in the heat. So, I get
the summer takes long to end, goes out
in a swan song of trees, trunks water
witch light from the sun, fritter into

space with thoughts of a bleached blond
struck dumb. Finally, each maple, oak,
steps out from the gang of green, shows
true colours, leaves the youth crowd behind.

Not in Stone

Homes flimsy as toy matchstick houses,
an autumn's flame of trees could set
alight. Not in stone, not set down for

the permanence of centuries. Something
learned in the journey, everything fixed
in European culture left. The white cloud

of smoke flees the brick chimney, fills
the sky with a spread map. A sail pulls
a craft into a day. The sea's swell gave

a desire for straight lines, planks to
align, to make the side of a saltbox not
tilt, learnt from a see sawing horizon,

the motion of days at sea. The 12 x 12
windows, a grid to map an ocean when
a wave of leaves splash the wooden hull.

Carcass

Better to be back before
the trees turn to scarecrows,
trail stuffing they can't keep.

Better to be here before leaves
fly about them, like birds
the effigies send away.

Better we all be scared
by what we can't keep.
Better to be crow-ready,

scavenge the year's
carcass, as it stiffens
and fritters away.

Damper

The trees pass out tracts on death.
Starve themselves to be an example,
strip off their St Francis rags.

We are all poor this time of year,
when leaves shed a calendar of days,
lead sheet by sheet to the great

white void. The heavy descent of
marble chips. Ivory weighted piano
keys press down icy fingers.

So plants rise, rise: hammers
hit strings in a field's taut furrow
as a damper slacks off the land.

Un-Plug the Tree

Let it twirl out from the string of lights,
a top spins to the edge of the room.

Unplug from the socket, dented pig's snout.
Pick up broken glass ornaments, apples

bitten into, discarded at a feast with
too many choices. Known as she-balsam

milked for resin, nursed presents, bows
soft as ears under a branch. Now tilts,

tipsy as a late-night party hat. Has another
life waiting outside, will drop needles one by

one into a golden haystack like a seamstress
loses pins as she trims a one night stand frock.

Unpacking the Tree

This year it is Caesarean style,
I cut the box open regardless
of the silver steel stitching on
the side from a previous

operation. The brown cardboard
hacked and piled up in mounds
as if I dug through dirt to
uproot it. Branches crosshatched

like laces on an old shoe. I cut
the green strings and it moves
into a new step, a ballerina
changes from first to second

position. It is fragrance which
will adorn our lives. Frankin-
cense, myrrh announced portly
midnight guests. It sits rotund, wise.

Christmas Week, Washington CT

The bare apple trees in Averill's
Orchard contort like Pilobolus
Dancers in one of their performances.

The Congregational Church with
its spire is an origami sculpture,
folded white, neatens into a holiness

of angles. I see a man kneeling
before a maple tapping it in
December like a pilgrim waits

for some stigmata. The season's warmth
unpredictable, everything reveals
a new form as the earth unwraps layers.

Snake Skin

We all leave traces of ourselves,
the old blouse in the dryer circles,

a hamster in a cage. Strips of skin
on the stone walk, flat as condoms.

One dribbles from the wall, saliva
from a mouth, Moses parched water

emits from stone. Like a train rushes
through a tunnel, the serpent comes

out on time. The repeated shedding,
leaves a tape measure of what it was.

Thin wings of renewal, the inverse,
of shadow, an umbilical cord ripples light.

Silver tongued as ever, like the sword
guarding Eden flashes back and forth.

About the Author

Nancy Anne Miller is a Bermudian poet with six books: *Somersault* (*Guernica Editions* 2015), *Because There Was No Sea* (Anaphora Literary Press 2014), *Immigrant's Autumn* (Aldrich Press 2014). *Water Logged* (Aldrich Press 2016), *Star Map* (FutureCycle press 2016*). Island Bound Mail* (Kelsay Books 2017) Her poems have appeared *in Edinburgh Review (UK), Agenda (UK),Ambit (UK), Stand (UK),The International Literary Quarterly (UK), Magma (UK), Journal of Postcolonial Writing (UK), Wasafiri (UK), Mslexia (UK), New Welsh Review (UK), The Moth (IE),A New Ulster (IE), Southword Journal (IE), The Fiddlehead (CA), The Dalhousie Review (CA),The Toronto Quarterly blog (CA), Postcolonial Text (CA), Transnational Literatures (AU),The Caribbean Writer (VI), tongues of the ocean (BS),Sargasso: Journal of Caribbean Literature (PR), Bim (BB), Poui (BB), Moko: Caribbean Arts and Letters (TT), The Arts Journal (GY) The Pacuare Anthology (CR), Metaphor (PH), The Missing Slate (PK), The Open Road Review (IN), Papercuts (IN), Poetry Salzburg Review (AT), Proud Flesh: New Afrikan Journal of Culture, Politics, Consciousness USA), Journal of Caribbean Literatures (USA), St. Katherine's Review (USA), Hampton Sydney Poetry Review(USA), Theodate (USA) Free Verse: A Journal of Contemporary Poetry and Poetics* (USA), *Interviewing the Caribbean* (USA), among others. She has an M Litt in Creative Writing from Univ. of Glasgow, is a MacDowell Fellow, and is a three-time recipient of Bermuda Art Council Grants. She teaches poetry workshops in Bermuda and represented Bermuda in Poetry World Cup. She organized Ber-Mused, a poetry reading for BDA's 400 in 2009. She was shortlisted for the small axe salon (Caribbean) poetry prize (2013), guest edited *tongues of the ocean (BS),* and was included in *Arts Etc Barbados* (BB) tribute for Kamau Brathwaite. She resides in the bucolic Washington, CT.